Stay Wit' It

A 30-Day Motivational Detox for the Growing Woman

Alys Alexander

DEDICATION

For my loving and supportive parents,

Hopefully this makes up for that window I broke
Love you forever

ALYS ALEXANDER

Day One

Privately build it before publicly revealing it.
Don't get so caught up in "keeping up with the Jones"
that you prematurely divulge information. Timing is
everything.

Day Two

What God has for you will forever be yours.
Walk in your purpose knowing that no man nor
woman can ever take away what they did not give.
When it is God destined, it's guaranteed.

Day Three

Average < EXCEPTIONAL
Wake up every day with the mindset that you do not
have the capacity to sit around being average. Your
purpose is to be great, not mediocre. Nothing about
you is common, and that is the beauty of it.

Day Four

ALL BETS ON YOU!
*Be so confident in every aspect of you that you're
willing to risk it all. Why? Because that's how
powerful you really are. Remember female bees are
the only ones with the capability of stinging.*

Day Five

Easy? TUH! Girl please!
Stop praying for God to make things easier on you.
Instead ask for the strength to get through
everything coming your way. If He didn't think you
could handle it, He would have never chosen you.

Day Six

It's okay to be selfish. If it does not make you a better woman, increase your income, make you happy, or most importantly glorify God... LET IT GO! You have NO time for it.

Day Seven

Patience is key.
Many times, we expect things to happen when we feel
it's necessary, but that's not the case. Remember a
Toyota can be built in 13 hours, while a Rolls Royce
take six months. Exceptional quality requires
extensive exertion.

Day Eight

You don't have to advertise what's already known to be of high value.

I can bet that while watching television in your leisure, you haven't seen an Aston Martin, Ferrari, or Lamborghini commercial. Why? Because the individuals able to make such purchases are already aware of their value, and don't need a reminder. Nor are they sitting around watching television, but rather seeking ways to broaden their empire.

Day Nine

Be very cautious as to who you allow in your space (i.e. friends, associates, whom ever). Many people are just envious of who you are and what you have going on. It sickens them to see you win and pains them even more when they try to do what you've done, but fail.

Day Ten

Minding your business will forever be in style. There seems to be no traffic when you stay in your own lane. Only when you begin to veer off into a neighboring lane is when it gets a little crowded.

Day Eleven

You typically hear that "quitting is never an option."
That statement holds weight regarding many things,
however there are somethings you must
IMMEDIATELY quit doing. Quit trying to please
everyone; this is your life. Quit fearing change;
change is beautiful. Quit living in the past; you're
here for a reason. Quit putting yourself down; you're
everything and more. Quit overthinking; you have
someone in your corner that already has that
handled.

Day Twelve

Failure...There's No Such Thing.
If you never stop fighting for whatever it is that you
want, you can never fail, only get better. Whatever it
is that has you doubting your ability to keep going is
a lie, right along with the Devil. Rebuke it now!

Day Thirteen

We pray for the things we're unable to change and ask God to give us the answers to the things we don't understand. Sometimes the answer to the prayer is what you lose. So, count it all joy, because even though it seems like you took a loss, greater is coming! Losing the battle doesn't mean you've lost the war.

Day Fourteen

Change is a beautiful thing, but the first step to change is to recognize your own crap. Once you become aware of what it is you're doing wrong, take the necessary steps to fix it. Failure to do so will hinder your growth.

Day Fifteen

What you allow will continue. So don't complain about what you choose to make excuses for and allow in your life. You're in control of YOU.

Day Sixteen

We live in the world of "I don't get tired." and "I'll sleep when I'm dead." Getting tired is perfectly fine. Learn to rest, just do not quit.

Day Seventeen

Change your mindset. You must believe that success is your ONLY option.

Day Eighteen

Are you truly happy or just comfortable? Don't get complacent because it feels good. You're going to have to go through some turbulence to reach the higher altitudes. Settling is a no-no. If it isn't exactly what you've been fighting for, then why bother entertaining it?

Day Nineteen

What will people say?
How about, who cares what they say? Who cares
what they think or even how they feel? Who is THEY
anyways and who gave them the any authority? The
answer is no one! Do not contribute to the demise of
your own dreams. You're too smart to be the only
factor standing in your way.

Day Twenty

Feeling lonely, huh?
You've looked up and realized all those friends are
gone. God needs to seclude you from everyone else to
get your attention. Separation yields elevation;
everyone can't tag along. You'll appreciate it sooner
than you think.

Day Twenty- One

Baby, can you focus?
What distracting you? Who's standing in your way,
distorting your view? There comes a point when
you'll have to starve those distractions, and feed
your focus. If it isn't helping, it's hindering. Let the
intensity of your focus be so powerful that people
begin to question your sanity.

Day Twenty-Two

Pressure busts pipes!
Be willing to get a little uncomfortable. Staying in
your comfort zone won't yield the beauty of stepping
out of the box and taking some heat. Remember that
a diamond was once a chunk of coal that just did
well under pressure.

Day Twenty-Three

Selfishness is okay.
Invest your time into improving yourself, physically,
mentally, emotionally, financially and spiritually.
Pour into yourself so that you're able to pour into
others. You can't pour from an empty vessel.

Day Twenty-Four

You've Seen Worse
Recall your past. There were some situations you
thought you'd never overcome, right? Bouncing back
seemed impossible, but amid your suffering came
that breakthrough. Whatever it is right now, you'll
conquer it as well. Someone somewhere is depending
on you to get through this.

Day Twenty-Five

Their Eyes Were Watching ~~God~~ YOU!
Even if they do not like you, they'll forever be
watching. They'll hate your every being, yet
meticulously notate your every move. So allow them
to watch, don't block them out. God is preparing a
table before you in the presence of your enemies.

Day Twenty-Six

CAUTION! Threat Detected!
They will stop talking to you, but your name will constantly come up. Why? It is because you're doing something right. You posed a threat; your vision greatly differed from that of theirs. Keep doing what you're doing darling. The sight of your success and happiness sickens them. They're upset; they prayed for your downfall and are now seeking reimbursements.

Day Twenty-Seven

It's Going to Cost Ya!
The woman you're destined to be will not develop
overnight. You'll have to endure some losses. It is
going to hurt sometimes. However, you must
remember to choose her, always. She's worth it all.
You owe it to yourself.

Day Twenty-Eight

Protect Your P's

PEACE.

POSITIVE ENERGY.

PROGRESSION.

If there be anything removing your focus from the protection of these three factors, remove it immediately. Without these P's, you will find yourself leading a life of perpetual pity. Do it for you.

Day Twenty-Nine

Silence is GOLDEN.
Growth is a beautiful thing. You begin to realize
that you don't owe anyone anything. You aren't
seeking revenge, and you could care less about
getting the last word. Going tit for tat has become
nonexistent. Take your mental notes and allow
people to write themselves out of your life without
saying a word.

Day Thirty

They Ask You Who You Do It For...
You must be willing to do this for you. This isn't for
anyone else. Honor YOU. Love YOU. Cherish YOU.
Live for YOU. Never forget that you too are
priority. Choose more life. Choose living on purpose,
living your purpose. Forget habitually living day to
day. Be unapologetically intentional in all you do.

JOURNAL

_____

_____

_____

_____

_____

_____

_____

_____

_____

_____

_____

_____

_____

_____

_____

_____

_____

_____

_____

ALYS ALEXANDER

48

_____

_____

_____

_____

_____

_____

_____

_____

_____

_____

_____

_____

_____

_____

_____

_____

_____

_____

_____

_____

_____

_____

_____

_____

_____

_____

_____

_____

_____

_____

_____

_____

_____

_____

_____

_____

_____

_____

_____

_____

_____

_____

_____

_____

_____

_____

_____

_____

_____

_____

_____

_____

_____

_____

_____

_____

_____

_____

_____

_____

_____

_____

_____

_____

_____

_____

_____

_____

_____

_____

_____

_____

_____

_____

_____

_____

_____

_____

_____

_____

_____

_____

_____

_____

_____

_____

_____

_____

_____

_____

_____

_____

_____

_____

_____

_____

_____

_____

_____

_____

_____

_____

_____

_____

_____

_____

_____

_____

_____

_____

_____

_____

_____

_____

_____

_____

_____

_____

_____

_____

_____

_____

_____

_____

_____

_____

_____

_____

_____

_____

_____

_____

_____

_____

_____

_____

_____

_____

_____

_____

_____

_____

_____

_____

_____

_____

_____

_____

_____

_____

_____

_____

_____

_____

_____

_____

_____

_____

_____

_____

_____

Made in the USA
San Bernardino, CA
14 August 2019